CHANDLER, Fiona

Usborne first encyclopedia
of the human body

Usborne
First
Encyclopedia
of the
Human Body

Fiona Chandler

Designed by Susie McCaffrey

Illustrated by David Hancock and John Woodcock

Consultant: Dr. Kristina Routh

Using Internet links

Throughout this book we have recommended websites where you can find out more about the human body. To visit the sites, go to the Usborne Quicklinks Website where you will find links to all the sites.

1. Go to **www.usborne-quicklinks.com**
2. Type the keywords for this book: **first human body**
3. Type the page number of the link you want to visit.
4. Click on the links to go to the recommended sites.

Here are some of the things you can do on the websites recommended in this book:
• Watch a movie about your brain and nerves
• Try online activities about bones and skeletons
• See an animation of a heart beating
• Find facts, games and activities about genes
• See how people change as they age

Site availability

The links in Usborne Quicklinks are regularly reviewed and updated, but occasionally you may get a message that a site is unavailable. This might be temporary, so try again later, or even the next day. Websites do occasionally close down and when this happens, we will replace them with new links in Usborne Quicklinks. Sometimes we add extra links too, if we think they are useful. So when you visit Usborne Quicklinks, the links may be slightly different from those described in your book.

Downloadable pictures

Pictures marked with a ★ in this book can be downloaded from the Usborne Quicklinks Website. These pictures are for personal use only and must not be used for commercial purposes.

Safety on the Internet

Ask your parent's or guardian's permission before you connect to the Internet and make sure you follow these simple rules:

• Never give out information about yourself, such as your real name, address, phone number or the name of your school.

• If a site asks you to log in or register by typing your name or email address, ask permission from an adult first

What you need

To visit the websites you need a computer with an Internet connection and a web browser (the software that lets you look at information from the Internet). Some sites need extra programs (plug-ins) to play sound or show videos or animations.

If you go to a site and do not have the necessary plug-in, a message will come up on the screen. There is usually a link to click on to download the plug-in. For more information about plug-ins, go to Usborne Quicklinks and click on "Net Help".

Notes for parents and guardians

The websites described in this book are regularly reviewed, but the content of a website may change at any time and Usborne Publishing is not responsible for the content on any website other than its own.

We recommend that children are supervised while on the Internet, that they do not use Internet chat rooms, and that you use Internet filtering software to block unsuitable material. Please ensure that your children read and follow the safety guidelines printed above. For more information, see the Net Help area on the Usborne Quicklinks Website

Contents

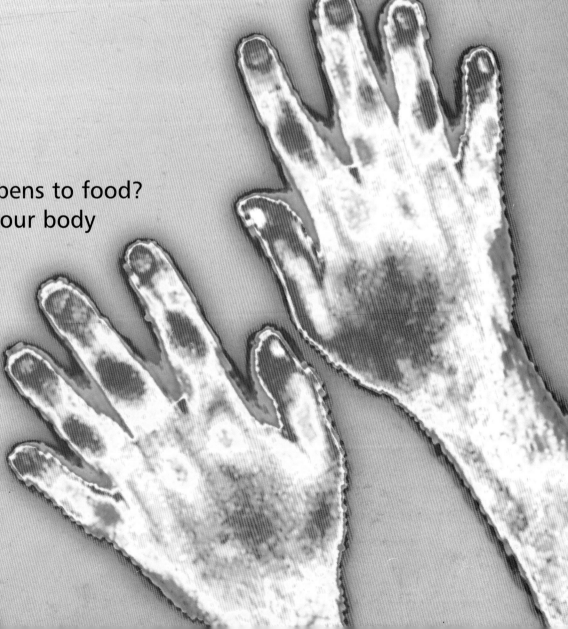

This is a special kind of photo that shows how hot or cold things are. The warmest parts show up white or red.

Inside your body

Your body is like an amazingly complicated machine. It is made up of lots of different parts. All of them work together to help you stay alive.

Small cells

Your body is made of millions and millions of tiny living cells. Most of your cells are much too small to see. Scientists have to look at them through a machine called a microscope.

Some of the biggest cells in your body are only the size of these tiny dots.

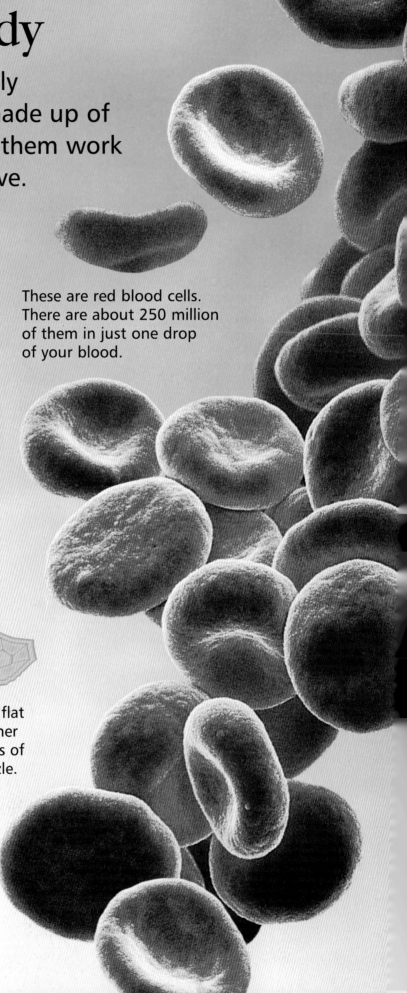

These are red blood cells. There are about 250 million of them in just one drop of your blood.

Cell shapes

There are many different shapes and sizes of body cells. Each kind does a different job. Here are just a few of them.

★ Fat cells are round, like balls.

★ Skin cells are flat and fit together like the pieces of a jigsaw puzzle.

★ Muscle cells are long and thin.

★ Some nerve cells are shaped like trees.

Body parts

Millions of cells join together to make all the parts of your body. Important body parts, such as your brain, heart and stomach, are called organs. Each organ has its own job to do.

This picture shows some of the main organs in your body.

Internet link ✋

For a link to a website where you can play a game to see what jobs different parts of your body do, go to **www.usborne-quicklinks.com**

Staying alive

To stay alive, your body needs food, water, and air to breathe. Air contains a gas called oxygen that all your cells need to keep them working.

Your brain runs your body and sends instructions to all your other organs.

Your heart pumps blood around your body.

★

Your lungs breathe in air.

Your liver cleans your blood.

Your stomach holds food.

Your intestines break down food for your body to use.

★ Food helps you grow and gives you energy to move around.

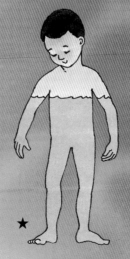

★ Two-thirds of your body is made up of water.

Your brain and nerves

Your brain controls everything that happens inside you. It sends out messages that tell all the other parts of your body what to do. These messages travel along your nerves.

Brain work

Your brain is working all the time. Even when you're fast asleep, it makes your heart beat and keeps you breathing. It's also the part of you that thinks, learns, makes decisions and remembers things.

Here you can see how your brain is linked to nerves all over your body.

Your spinal cord is a thick bundle of nerves that runs down your back.

Your other nerves are shown here in green.

The pale yellow lines are folds in the surface of the brain.

By the time you are six years old, your brain is as big as an adult's.

This is the skull. It's the bony part of the head that protects the brain.

This scan shows inside a person's head. The brain is the pale pink and yellow area.

The spinal cord links the brain to the rest of the body.

Sending messages

Your nerves carry messages to and from your brain. They let your brain know what is happening in the world around you. They also pass on instructions from your brain to the rest of your body.

Here's what happens when you catch a ball. All of this takes just a fraction of a second.

1. You see a ball coming to you. Your nerves pass this message from your eyes to your brain.

2. Your brain decides to catch the ball. It sends a message to tell your arms to move.

3. Nerves carry the message to your arms and hands. They move to catch the ball.

Internet link

For a link to a website where you can watch a movie to find out lots more about your brain and nerves, go to **www.usborne-quicklinks.com**

Speedy cells

Your brain and nerves are made of millions of nerve cells, called neurons. When you think, electrical signals zoom around from neuron to neuron inside your brain.

Did you know?

• The neurons that reach from your spinal cord to your toes are the longest cells in your body. They can grow to over 1m (3ft) long.

• Messages whizz along your neurons at over 400kph (250mph).

• Each neuron in your brain can receive more than 100,000 messages every second.

Inside your brain, you have millions of tiny neurons like these.

7

Seeing

You use your eyes to see what's happening around you. You see things because light bounces off them and goes into your eyes. Your eyes send messages to your brain, which turns them into pictures you can see.

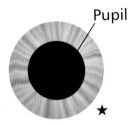

Pupil

When it's dark, your pupils get bigger to let in as much light as possible.

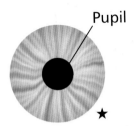

Pupil

In bright light, your pupils get smaller to stop too much light from getting in.

Follow the numbers to see what happens inside one of your eyes when you look at a flower.

1. Light bounces off the flower.

2. The light goes in through your pupil (the black dot in the middle of your eye).

3. This part of your eye, called the lens, bends the light so it points at the back of your eye.

4. An upside-down picture lands on your retina (the back wall of your eye). Special cells turn the picture into a message.

This is a close-up photo of the special cells at the back of your eye. You have about 136 million of them in each eye.

5. Nerves take the message to your brain. Your brain turns the picture the right way up and you "see" the flower.

Lashes and lids

Your eyes are very delicate and are easily damaged. Most of your eyeball is hidden inside your skull. The front of your eye is protected by your eyelids and eyelashes.

When you blink, your eyelids wipe tears across your eyes. This keeps them clean.

Your eyelids close instantly if anything comes near your eyes.

Internet links

For links to websites where you can try out lots of amazing activities to trick your eyes, go to **www.usborne-quicklinks.com**

Your eyelashes help to keep out dust.

The coloured part of your eye is called the iris.

Eye problems

Lots of people need glasses or contact lenses to help them see clearly. Short-sighted people need glasses to see things that are far away. Long-sighted people need glasses to see things that are close.

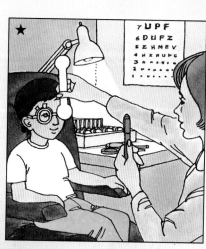

This boy is having his eyes tested by an optician to find out if he needs glasses.

Seeing colours

1. Take some crayons into a room at night. Turn out the lights and wait until you can see a little.

2. Look at the crayons. Can you tell what colours they are?

The cells in your eyes that pick up colours don't work in dim light. That's why it's hard to tell the crayons apart.

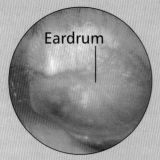

Eardrum

This is what a doctor sees when he looks inside your ear.

Hearing

Sit quietly for a moment and listen. What can you hear? Your ears can pick up thousands of different sounds, from the buzzing of a bee to the roar of a motorbike.

How you hear

Sounds make tiny particles in the air wobble, or vibrate. The vibrations travel through the air in invisible waves. You hear when these vibrations hit your ears.

Internet links

For links to websites where you can watch an animation that shows how the ear works and try a sound puzzle, go to **www.usborne-quicklinks.com**

★ Follow the numbers to see what happens inside one of your ears when you hear a sound.

1. The outside part of your ear collects the vibrations and funnels them inside.

2. The vibrations hit a patch of very thin skin, called your eardrum. They make it vibrate.

3. These tiny bones pass the vibrations on.

4. This part of your ear is filled with liquid. The vibrations make ripples in the liquid.

5. Inside here, nerve cells feel the ripples. They send a sound message to your brain.

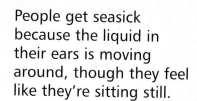

Nerve cell

The pink hair shapes in this microscope photo are nerve cells inside your ear. They bend when vibrations hit them.

Blowing into a trumpet makes the air inside it vibrate. High notes make fast vibrations and low notes make slow ones.

The vibrations come out here and travel through the air.

Two ears

You need both of your ears to work out where a sound is coming from. A sound that comes from your right hits your right ear first. It's also slightly louder in your right ear. Your brain notices this and tells you where the sound is coming from.

Balancing act

Your ears also help you to keep your balance. Inside each ear, there are tiny tubes with liquid in them. When you move your head, the liquid sloshes around inside the tubes. This tells your brain your head is moving.

When you spin around and around, the liquid in your ears keeps swirling around even after you've stopped. This makes you feel dizzy.

★ People get seasick because the liquid in their ears is moving around, though they feel like they're sitting still.

Taste and smell

Imagine if pizza and chocolate tasted the same. Or if you couldn't smell your dinner cooking. Without taste and smell, you wouldn't be able to enjoy your food.

Smells can warn you of danger. If you smell smoke, you know something's burning.

Nose job

Smells are tiny particles that float off things and go up your nose. High inside your nose, there's a patch of tiny, hair-like nerve cells. They sense the smell particles and send a message to your brain.

This shows what happens inside your nose when you smell a flower.

Nerves in here carry a smell message to your brain.

These are nerve cells that can sense smells.

Smell particles float into the air.

This big empty space is called your nasal cavity.

Tongue

Smell particles go in through your nostrils.

Tongue tasks

On your tongue, you have almost 10,000 tiny taste buds. They are made of special cells that can detect a few simple tastes. They tell your brain if your food is sweet, sour, salty or bitter.

Lemons are sour.

Coffee is bitter.

Crisps are salty.

Cake is sweet.

Close up, the surface of your tongue looks like this. The big, red circles have taste buds inside them, which can detect some simple tastes.

Internet link

For a link to a website where you can find out lots more about your nose, tongue and taste buds, go to **www.usborne-quicklinks.com**

Team work

When you eat, smell particles from your food float from the back of your throat up into your nose. This means that your nose actually helps you to taste things!

When you have a cold, your food tastes strange. This is because your nose gets blocked up and you can't smell properly.

Test your taste buds

You will need:
grated apple, grated pear and grated carrot in three separate bowls; a blindfold

1. Put on the blindfold and hold your nose.

2. Ask a friend to feed you a spoonful from each of the three bowls. Can you tell which food is which?

3. Try the same thing again without holding your nose. This time, it should be much easier to tell the foods apart.

Touch

When you touch something, your skin tells you what it feels like. Try running your fingers over this page. Does it feel rough or smooth?

In this picture, the part of your brain that deals with touch is shown in yellow.

Your skin is so sensitive that you can feel something as light as a butterfly resting on your finger.

Skin sensors

There are millions of tiny nerve endings, or sensors, in your skin. They can feel heat, cold, pressure, roughness or smoothness, and pain. They send touch messages zooming along nerve cells to your brain.

Some sensors work when you stroke things very gently. They let you feel a rabbit's soft, smooth fur.

Other sensors detect stronger pressure. When you squeeze a ball, they tell you if it is hard or squashy.

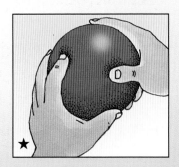

Some skin sensors feel heat and others feel cold. Which sensors do you think are working here?

If you cut yourself, pain sensors tell your brain it hurts.

14

Sensitive spots

Some parts of your body are better at feeling things than others. This is because they have far more touch sensors than other body parts.

Your lips and tongue are very sensitive. That's why babies like to feel things with their mouths.

You have more than 3,000 sensors in each fingertip.

Internet links

For links to websites where you can explore your sense of touch and send an interactive postcard, go to
www.usborne-quicklinks.com

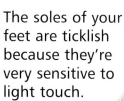

The soles of your feet are ticklish because they're very sensitive to light touch.

Why do things hurt?

Pain is very important. It warns you that something is wrong. If you touch something hot, it really hurts, so you pull your hand away as fast as you can. This stops you from getting too badly burned.

If you prick yourself, germs can get in. Pain warns you that your skin is damaged. ★

Test your touch sensors

You will need:
a blindfold; some similar-shaped objects, such as an apple, an onion, an orange and a tennis ball

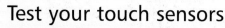

1. Place the objects on a table in front of you. Put on the blindfold.

2. Try feeling each of the objects with your elbow. Can you tell which one is which?

3. Now feel the objects with your fingers. Are fingers or elbows better at feeling things?

Skin

Your skin is like a thin, stretchy, waterproof coat. It protects your insides and keeps out dirt and germs. It also stops you from getting too hot or too cold.

The outside of your skin is made up of flat, flaky cells like these.

Dead or alive

The skin you can see is actually dead. New skin cells grow underneath and slowly push their way up to the surface. As they move up, they die. After a while, the dead cells fall off.

Your skin is made up of two main layers. This shows what's inside.

Hair

This is a touch sensor that can feel hot, cold or pain.

New skin cells grow here.

The top layer of skin is called the epidermis.

This tiny hole is called a pore.

The layer underneath is called the dermis.

Blood vessels

This is a sweat gland. It makes a salty liquid, called sweat.

This is a sebaceous gland. It makes oil that keeps your skin soft.

Tiny tubes, called blood vessels, carry blood to your skin.

★ Beneath your skin, there's a layer of fat cells.

Keeping cool

When it's hot, sweat glands in your skin make more sweat. As the sweat dries, it takes heat away from your body and cools you down.

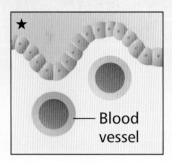

When you get hot, the blood vessels in your skin get wider. This lets more blood into your skin.

The extra blood makes you look red. But it lets the air around you cool your blood down faster.

Blood vessel

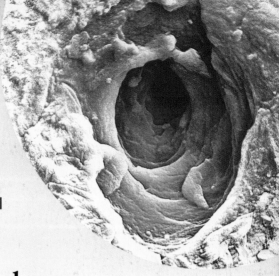

Sweat oozes out through pores, like this one. You have about three million sweat pores all over your skin.

Internet links

For links to websites where you can explore the skin on your arm and find out lots of fun skin facts, go to **www.usborne-quicklinks.com**

Skin and sun

Some of your skin cells make a brown colouring called melanin. Melanin helps to protect your skin from sunlight. It also gives your skin its colour. Dark-skinned people have lots of melanin in their skin. Light-skinned people only have a little.

If you're in the sun a lot, your skin makes more melanin, so it gets darker.

Too much sunlight can damage your skin. When it's very sunny, it's a good idea to cover up and rub in lots of sunscreen.

Hair and nails

Your hair and nails are actually made of the same stuff. It's called keratin and there's lots of it in your skin too. Like your skin, your hair and nails are mostly dead.

All about hair

You have millions of hairs on your body, but many of them are too short and fine to see. The longest, thickest hairs are on your head. They keep heat in and help to stop your head from getting sunburned.

This close-up photo shows how hair grows deep inside your skin.

You have no hair at all in these places.

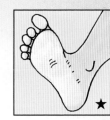

Lips

Palms of the hands

Soles of the feet

This part is called the hair shaft.

Surface of the skin

Each hair grows out of a tiny tube, called a follicle.

This is the hair root. New hair cells grow here. It's the only part of the hair that's alive.

Did you know?

• Your hair grows about 1.2cm (½in) every month.

• Most people's hair stops growing when it gets to about 60cm (2ft).

• You have about 100,000 hairs on your head.

• Up to 100 hairs fall out of your head every day.

Like your skin, your hair contains a colouring called melanin. Blond hair has much less melanin in it than dark hair.

Straight or curly?

It's the shape of your hairs that makes them straight or curly.

Straight hairs are a round shape. ★

Wavy hairs are oval. ★

Curly hairs are flat. ★

Internet links 🖐

For links to websites where you can watch a short movie about hair and find out lots more fascinating facts about your hair and nails, go to **www.usborne-quicklinks.com**

Hard as nails

Your nails protect the ends of your fingers and toes. Your fingernails also help you to pick things up. If you don't cut your nails, they keep on growing. The longest thumbnail ever was an amazing 1m (3ft) long.

This shows underneath a nail.

This part of the nail is dead.

The part under the nail is called the nail bed.

★ New nail cells grow in the nail root.

Bones

You have over 200 bones inside you. They support your body and hold you up. Without them, you'd just be a shapeless blob.

Your skeleton

Together, your bones make up your skeleton. It acts as a framework for your whole body.

Bones protect your organs. The rib bones in your chest stop your heart and lungs from getting squashed.

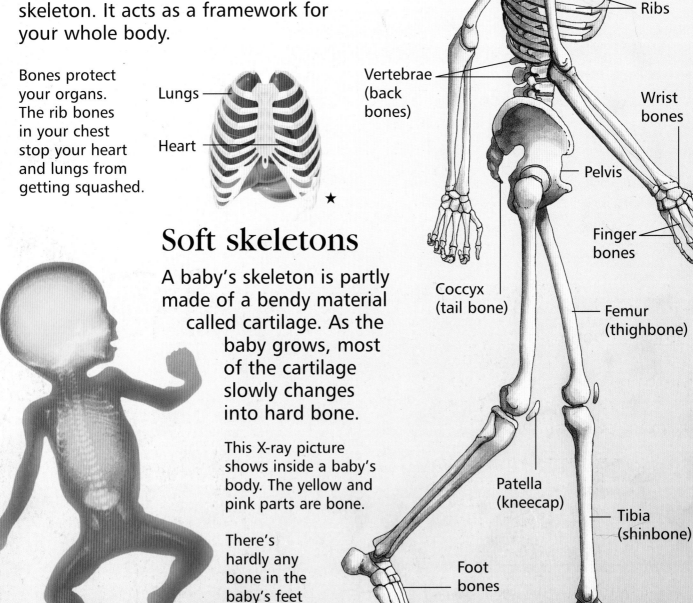

Lungs

Heart

★

This is a grown-up's skeleton with some of its main bones named.

Shoulder blade

Skull

Jawbone

Collarbone

Breast-bone

Ribs

Vertebrae (back bones)

Wrist bones

Pelvis

Finger bones

Coccyx (tail bone)

Femur (thighbone)

Patella (kneecap)

Tibia (shinbone)

Foot bones

Toe bones

★

Soft skeletons

A baby's skeleton is partly made of a bendy material called cartilage. As the baby grows, most of the cartilage slowly changes into hard bone.

This X-ray picture shows inside a baby's body. The yellow and pink parts are bone.

There's hardly any bone in the baby's feet and hands.

In your bones

Your bones are alive, just like the softer parts of your body. Inside each bone, there are millions of living cells. The cells produce a stony substance that makes your bones strong and hard.

Your thighbone is the biggest bone in your body. This is what it looks like inside.

★

Blood vessel

This is a kind of bone called compact bone. It is very strong.

The middle is filled with fatty stuff, called bone marrow.

This is spongy bone. It has lots of holes inside it.

Internet links

For links to websites with online activities about bones and skeletons, go to **www.usborne-quicklinks.com**

Broken bones

Although bones are strong, they sometimes get broken. When this happens, the cells inside slowly grow to join the broken ends together again.

★

A hard plaster cast holds the bone in the right place until it mends.

Doctors use X-ray pictures to look at bones. This is an X-ray of a broken arm.

The bones are broken here.

Joints

Joints are places where bones meet. They let your body bend and move into different positions.

Here you can see some of the main joints in the body.

How joints work

Your bones are held together by tough straps, called ligaments. The end of each bone is covered with smooth, shiny cartilage. This allows the bones to slide against each other.

This is what your knee joint looks like inside.

Ankle joint

Stretching makes joints more bendy, or supple. Gymnasts have very supple joints.

Knee joint

The back is made up of lots of different bones, with joints between them.

Hip joint

Shoulder joint

Elbow joint

Wrist joint

Kneecap

Thighbone

Cartilage

Ligament

Cartilage

The joint is filled with slippery liquid to keep it working smoothly.

Shinbone

★

Kinds of joints

You have different kinds of joints that let you move in different ways. Some, like your hip, can move in a big circle. Others, like your knee, can only move up and down.

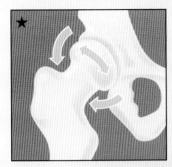

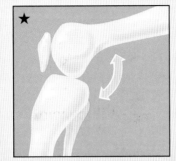

Your hip joint looks like this. The round end of one bone fits into a cup-shaped socket in the other.

Your knee works like a door hinge. It can move up and down, but it can't move from side to side.

Why do you need joints?

Try moving around without bending your knees and elbows. Now try sitting down. Can you get up again?

If you had no joints at all, you wouldn't be able to move.

Internet links

For links to websites where you can see how different joints move, and turn a chicken bone into rubber, go to
www.usborne-quicklinks.com

Joint problems

Sometimes, a joint gets dislocated. This means that the bones get pushed out of place, so they don't meet any more. A doctor has to pull them back into place before the joint can heal.

This X-ray picture shows a dislocated elbow.

The arm bones should meet here.

Upper arm bone

This bone has slipped out of place.

Lower arm bones

23

Muscles

Most of your muscles are joined to bones. They make your body move. Without them, you couldn't walk, run, speak – or even breathe.

Internet links

For links to websites where you can watch animations and try fun activities about muscles, go to **www.usborne-quicklinks.com**

There are over 600 muscles in your body. This picture shows some of the main ones.

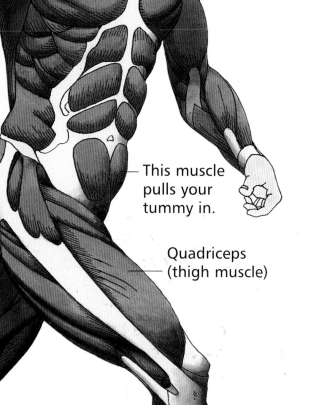

This muscle lets you shrug your shoulders.

This muscle wrinkles your forehead.

Triceps

Deltoid (shoulder muscle)

Biceps

This muscle pulls your tummy in.

Quadriceps (thigh muscle)

This is a tendon. Tendons join muscles to bones.

Calf muscle

Pulling power

Muscles work by tightening up and getting shorter. When a muscle tightens, it pulls on the bones it's joined to and makes them move. Muscles can only pull, so you need two different muscles to bend and straighten a joint.

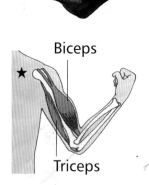

Biceps

Triceps

Biceps

Triceps

To bend your arm, the biceps muscle tightens, pulling up your lower arm.

To straighten your arm, the triceps muscle tightens, pulling your lower arm down.

Feel your muscles

1. Place your hand gently around your upper arm.

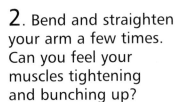

2. Bend and straighten your arm a few times. Can you feel your muscles tightening and bunching up?

The muscles in your face pull on your skin to make you smile or frown.

Body heat

When muscles work, they give off heat. This helps to keep your body warm. When you run around, your muscles have to work harder and they give off even more heat. That's why you get hot when you exercise.

When you need to warm up, your brain tells your muscles to move, and you shiver.

Marvellous muscles

Some special muscles work without you even thinking about them. The muscles in your heart keep it beating all the time, even when you're asleep – and they never get tired.

Muscles are made up of long, thin cells, called muscle fibres. This is a close-up photo of muscle fibres in the heart.

Exercise makes your muscles grow bigger. Athletes train hard to keep their muscles strong.

25

Blood

Blood flows around inside you all the time. It carries food and a gas called oxygen to all your body's cells.

What is blood?

Blood is made up of different kinds of cells that do different jobs. The blood cells float in a watery, yellow liquid, called plasma. Plasma is the part of your blood that carries food.

An adult human body contains about 5 litres (9 pints) of blood. That's roughly the same as 15 cans of cola.

Internet links

For links to websites where you can find out all about blood with fun animations and activities, go to **www.usborne-quicklinks.com**

You have three kinds of blood cells in your body. This is what they look like under a microscope.

White blood cells kill germs that get inside your body. They help to stop you from getting ill.

Platelets are tiny parts of cells. They stop you bleeding if you cut yourself.

Red blood cells carry oxygen around your body. They give your blood its colour.

How blood travels

Your heart pumps blood around your body. The blood travels along thousands of tubes, called blood vessels. Blood vessels that take blood away from your heart are called arteries. Those that take blood back to your heart are called veins.

This picture shows some of the main arteries and veins in your body.

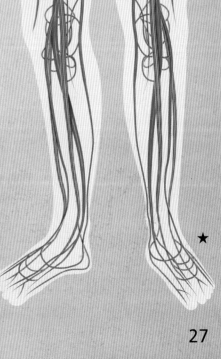

Heart

Vein

This big artery takes blood to the lower part of your body.

Did you know?

• One drop of your blood contains about 250 million red blood cells, 13 million platelets and 375,000 white blood cells.

• Every day, your blood travels about 15km (over 9 miles) around your body.

Clots and scabs

If you cut yourself, blood vessels get broken and blood leaks out. Right away, the platelets in your blood get to work to stop you bleeding. These pictures show what happens.

Surface of the skin

Platelet

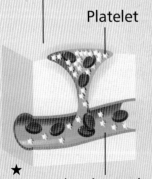

★

Blood vessel

Red blood cell

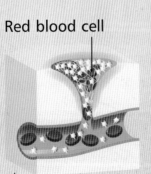

★

Scab

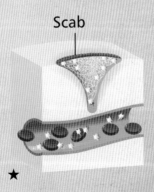

★

1. The platelets clump together around the cut. This helps to plug up the leak.

2. The platelets help make a sticky net to trap red blood cells. A jelly-like clot forms.

3. The clot dries to form a hard scab. Underneath, new cells grow and the cut heals.

Your heart

Your heart is only about the size of your fist, but it's very strong. It pumps blood to every part of your body.

Body pump

Your heart is made of muscle that tightens and relaxes all the time. When your heart relaxes, it lets blood in. When it tightens, it squeezes the blood out again. This is your heart "beating".

Heart valve open   Heart valve closed

This is a gate, or valve, inside your heart. The thump of your heartbeat is the sound of the valves snapping shut.

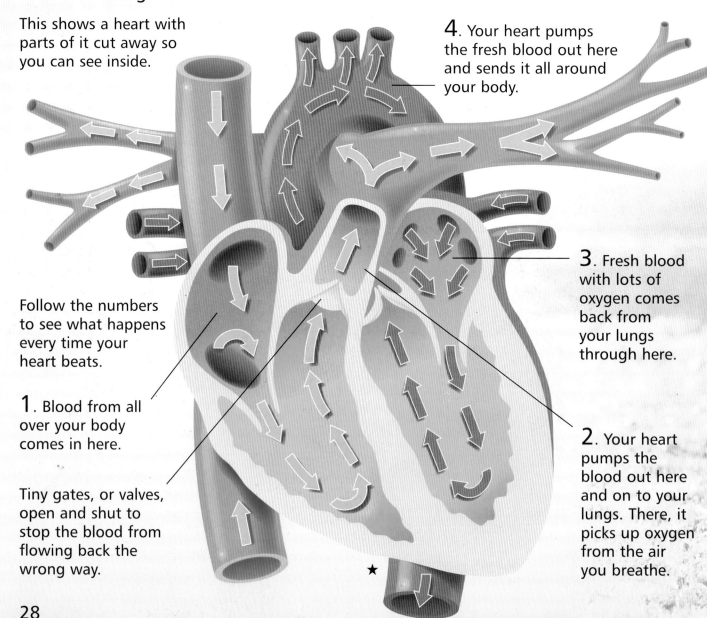

This shows a heart with parts of it cut away so you can see inside.

4. Your heart pumps the fresh blood out here and sends it all around your body.

3. Fresh blood with lots of oxygen comes back from your lungs through here.

Follow the numbers to see what happens every time your heart beats.

1. Blood from all over your body comes in here.

Tiny gates, or valves, open and shut to stop the blood from flowing back the wrong way.

2. Your heart pumps the blood out here and on to your lungs. There, it picks up oxygen from the air you breathe.

28

Feel your pulse

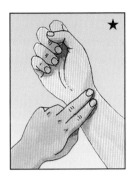

To feel your blood being pumped around your body, press two fingers on the inside of your wrist. The beating you can feel is called your pulse.

How fast?

When you're sitting still, your heart beats more than 70 times every minute. It beats harder and faster when you exercise.

Exercising makes your heart work harder. This keeps it healthy.

Here you can see a person's heart. The red and yellow lines are blood vessels.

When you run around, your muscles need more food and oxygen. Your heart speeds up so it can pump blood around your body faster.

Heart problems

The outside of your heart is covered in blood vessels. They keep your heart muscles alive. In older people, the blood vessels sometimes get blocked, so the muscles can't work properly. This is called a heart attack.

Internet link

For a link to a website where you can see a moving picture of blood flowing through the heart, go to **www.usborne-quicklinks.com**

Breathing

Without thinking about it, you breathe in and out about 23,000 times a day. When you breathe, you take in oxygen from the air. All your body's cells need oxygen to stay alive.

How you breathe

Under your lungs, you have a big muscle called your diaphragm (say "die-a-fram"). You also have muscles between your ribs. You use all these muscles to breathe in and out.

Every time you breathe, you suck air into your lungs. Follow the arrows to see where the air goes.

Hairs inside your nose keep out big particles of dust.

This is your nasal cavity. Its sides are lined with sticky liquid that traps dirt and germs.

When you breathe in, your muscles tighten. Your chest gets bigger and your lungs take in air.

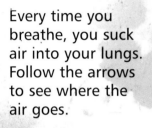

★

Throat

When you breathe out, your muscles relax. Your chest gets smaller and squeezes air out of your lungs.

This flap is called your epiglottis. When you swallow, it closes. This stops food from getting into your air tubes.

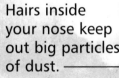

★

Windpipe

When you breathe in, air fills your lungs. They blow up like two balloons.

This is your diaphragm. It's a big sheet of muscle that helps you breathe.

★

Internet link

For a link to a website where you can find out how your heart and lungs work together, go to **www.usborne-quicklinks.com**

Windpipe

In your lungs

Inside, your lungs are full of tiny air tubes. The smallest tubes are no wider than a hair. The tubes end in little air bags surrounded by blood vessels. Oxygen passes from the air bags into your blood.

Each tiny tube has a bunch of air bags at the end of it.

This is what your lungs look like inside.

Close up, the air bags look like this.

Air bag

Blood vessels

How much air is in your lungs?

You will need:
a plastic bottle; a bendy straw; a bowl of water

1. Fill the bottle with water and put the lid on. Hold it upside down in the bowl and take the lid off.

 ★

2. Push the straw into the neck of the bottle. Take a deep breath, then blow gently into the straw until your lungs are empty.

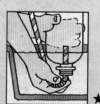 ★

3. All the air you breathe out gets trapped at the top of the bottle. This is how much air your lungs can hold.

 ★

Breathing problems

Some people have a condition called asthma that makes their air tubes suddenly get narrower. This makes it hard for them to breathe.

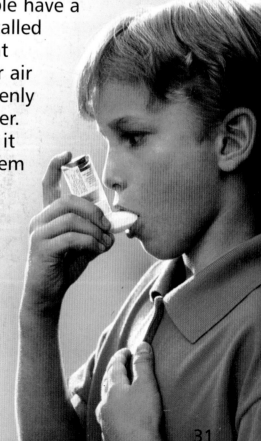

This boy is using an inhaler to breathe in medicine. This widens his air tubes, so he can breathe more easily.

Your voice

Think of all the sounds you can make with your voice. You can talk, whisper, shout, groan, scream, sing or hum. You use these sounds to tell people what you are thinking and feeling.

Babies can make sounds long before they can talk. They learn to say their first words when they're about a year old.

Making sounds

You make sounds in a part of your throat called your larynx. Inside it are two stretchy bands, called your vocal cords. Air from your lungs pushes up between your vocal cords and makes them wobble, or vibrate. You hear these vibrations as sounds.

This picture shows inside your throat and mouth.

This is your windpipe. Air from your lungs comes up here when you breathe out.

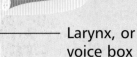

Teeth

Tongue

Larynx, or voice box

Vocal cords

★

Vocal cords

★

These are your vocal cords seen from above. When you are quiet, they stay open to let you breathe.

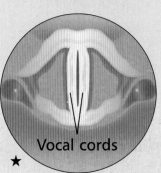

Vocal cords

★

When you make a sound, your vocal cords close. Air pushes through the tiny gap between them.

Mouth moves

When you talk or sing, you use your mouth as well as your vocal cords. You can make lots of different sounds by moving your lips and tongue.

Here you can see how the shape of your mouth changes to make different sounds.

"Ah"

"Ee"

"Oo"

Saying sounds

1. Say the sound "b". Do you use your tongue or your lips to make this sound?

2. Now say a "v" sound. Can you feel how your lips touch your teeth?

3. Now try saying a "d" sound. What does your tongue do?

Internet link

For a link to a website where you can see inside a woman's throat and watch her vocal cords moving as she sings, go to **www.usborne-quicklinks.com**

High or low?

As you grow up, your vocal cords get longer. This means they vibrate more slowly and your voice sounds lower. Men have longer and thicker vocal cords than women. That's why their voices are deeper.

When you speak or sing, your vocal cords tighten and relax. Tight vocal cords vibrate faster and make higher sounds.

When a woman sings a very high note, her vocal cords vibrate about 1,000 times a second.

Teeth

Imagine trying to eat an apple if you had no teeth. You use your teeth to cut up your food and crush it into small pieces that you can swallow.

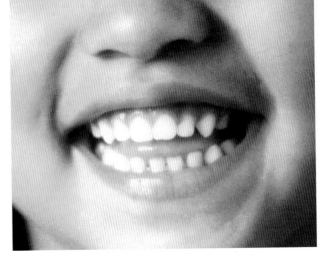

Your teeth have a tough, white covering, called enamel. Enamel is the hardest thing in your body.

Types of teeth

When you're little, you have 20 small teeth. They are called milk teeth or baby teeth. When you're about six years old, your milk teeth start to fall out. New, bigger teeth grow in their place. You will have these new teeth for the rest of your life.

Most grown-ups have 32 teeth. Different shapes of teeth do different jobs.

Sharp incisors are for biting off pieces of food.

Pointy canines can tear food.

Molars have a big, bumpy surface for chewing food.

This boy has lost some of his milk teeth. They were pushed out by bigger teeth growing underneath.

Premolars are smaller than molars, but they're good at chewing too.

Inside a tooth

The part of a tooth you can see is called the crown. Underneath, your teeth have long roots that fit into holes in your jawbone. Your teeth are very hard on the outside. But inside, they're soft – and they're alive.

This is what a tooth looks like inside.

Internet links

For links to websites where you'll find games, quizzes and songs to help you learn more about your teeth, go to **www.usborne-quicklinks.com**

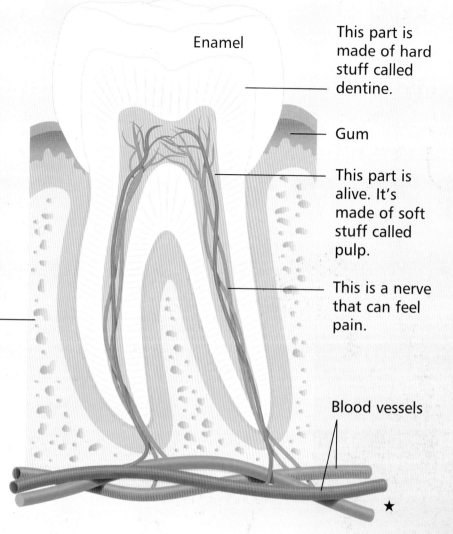

Enamel

This part is made of hard stuff called dentine.

Gum

This part is alive. It's made of soft stuff called pulp.

This is a nerve that can feel pain.

Jawbone

Blood vessels

Tooth care

Did you know you have lots of germs living inside your mouth? They feed on any sweet food stuck to your teeth. They also eat away at your teeth and make holes in them. Here's how you can keep your teeth healthy.

Don't eat or drink too many sweet things.

Brush your teeth at least twice a day to clean away any leftover food.

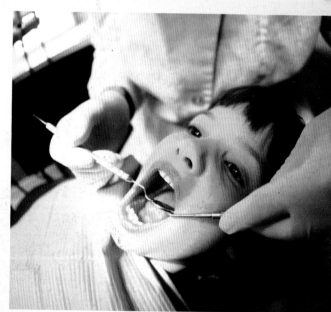

It's a good idea to visit a dentist regularly. Your dentist can check if your teeth are healthy and can show you how to clean them properly.

35

What happens to food?

You need food to stay alive. When you eat, your body has to turn your food into chemicals it can use. This is called digestion.

Your food's journey

Food takes between 18 and 48 hours to travel through your body. On the way, it gets broken down into smaller and smaller pieces. Follow the numbers on the big picture to see how this happens.

Internet link

For a link to a website where you can watch a movie that shows what happens to the food you eat, go to **www.usborne-quicklinks.com**

Salivary glands (where saliva is made)

Teeth

— Throat

— Gullet

1. As you chew your food, it mixes with saliva (spit). This makes it mushy and easy to swallow.

2. When you swallow, the food is pushed down your throat into a tube called your gullet.

3. Muscles in your gullet squeeze the food down into your stomach.

Did you know?

- A grown-up's salivary glands make about 1.5 litres (2½ pints) of saliva (spit) every day.

- Your stomach is only about as big as your fist, but it can stretch to 20 times that size.

- If a person's food tubes were stretched out, they would be as long as a bus.

4. Your stomach mashes up the food to make a thick liquid.

6. The food chemicals are taken to your liver, ready to be sent around your body.

Large intestine

5. Your small intestine turns the food into a runny soup. Then it takes out the food chemicals your body needs.

Rectum

8. The lumps of waste are squeezed out of your rectum when you go to the toilet.

7. Your large intestine collects food that you can't digest. It takes water out of it, leaving lumps of sludgy waste.

What's food for?

In your small intestine, food chemicals pass into your blood. Your blood carries this food to all your body's cells.

Some food gives your cells the energy they need to work. Some food is used to help you grow or to mend injuries, such as broken bones.

Your small intestine is lined with finger-like shapes like these. They have tiny blood vessels inside that take in chemicals from your food.

Waste disposal

Your body can't digest things like fruit skin and pips. They go into your large intestine and collect in sludgy lumps called faeces (poo). These lumps end up in the toilet.

Scraps of food

Water in your body

All your body's cells need water to work properly. Without water, you would only stay alive for a few days.

Water balance

To stay healthy, you need to keep the same amount of water in your body all the time. You lose water when you sweat and when you go to the toilet. You have to drink to put back the water you've lost.

To stay healthy, you should drink plenty of water every day.

You take in water in drinks and in food. Some foods are more than nine-tenths water.

When you feel thirsty, your body is telling you it needs more water.

See your breath

You lose a little water every time you breathe out. Try this to see for yourself.

Breathe gently onto a mirror. See how your breath makes a mist on the glass.

The mist is made up of tiny droplets of water that you've breathed out.

Internet link

For a link to a website where you can watch a movie that shows how your body gets rid of water it doesn't need, go to **www.usborne-quicklinks.com**

Waste water

Your kidneys control how much water is in your body. They get rid of any extra water that you don't need. They also clean your blood by taking out harmful chemicals made by your body's cells.

Your kidneys turn the extra water and chemicals into a liquid called urine (wee). Follow the numbers to see where the urine goes.

1. Your kidneys take out waste water and chemicals from your blood. They turn this into urine.

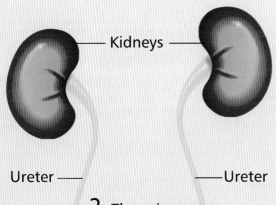

Kidneys

Ureter ——   —— Ureter

2. The urine trickles down two tubes, called ureters.

3. The urine goes into a stretchy bag, called your bladder.

Bladder

Urethra ——

4. When you go to the toilet, your bladder opens. The urine comes out of a tube called your urethra.

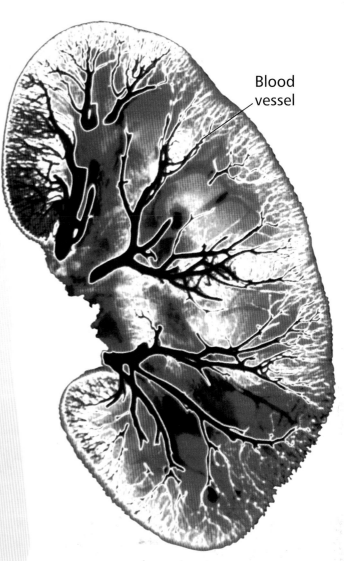

Blood vessel

Your kidneys clean all the blood in your body every four minutes. This X-ray photo shows inside a kidney.

Babies and toddlers can't control when they get rid of urine. That's why they have to wear nappies.

Hormones

Hormones are chemicals that travel around in your blood. They're like messengers that tell different parts of your body what to do.

Hormone jobs

Some hormones keep your body working properly. Some make you grow. Others change the way you look as you grow up. It's because of hormones that men and women look different.

As boys grow up, a male hormone makes hair grow on their faces.

Growth hormones make your body grow. That's why teenagers are taller than young children.

As girls grow up, female hormones make them grow breasts. Their bodies change so they can have babies.

If your blood gets too sugary, it makes you ill. A hormone called insulin stops this from happening, even when you eat sweet food.

People with an illness called diabetes can't make enough insulin. Some need to have injections of extra insulin every day.

Don't panic!

When you're scared, your body makes a hormone called adrenaline. It makes your heart beat faster and sends more blood to your muscles. This helps you to face danger – or run away if you have to.

If you go on a scary ride like a rollercoaster, your body makes lots of adrenaline. That's why going on rides feels so exciting.

Making hormones

Hormones come from small organs, called glands. The hormones ooze out of your glands and go into your blood.

Here are some of the main glands in your body.

Your pituitary gland makes growth hormones and controls lots of other glands.

Your thyroid gland controls how fast your body uses up energy.

Your adrenal glands make adrenaline.

Your pancreas makes insulin.

These are the ovaries. They make girls' female hormones.

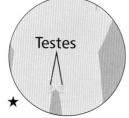

Testes

These are the testes. They make boys' male hormones.

Internet link

For a link to a website where you can find answers to common questions about diabetes, go to **www.usborne-quicklinks.com**

Genes

Look at yourself in a mirror for a moment. What colour are your eyes? Is your hair straight or curly? It's your genes that make you look the way you do.

Your genes decide lots of things about you. Here are just a few of them.

The colour of your eyes

The colour of your hair

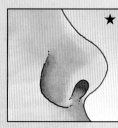
The shape of your nose

If you're left- or right-handed

How tall you grow

What are genes?

Genes are like a set of instructions that tell your body how to work and what shape to grow. Your genes are much too small to see, but they're inside almost every cell in your body.

Your genes are made of a chemical called DNA. It looks like a twisted ladder.

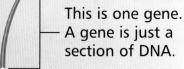
This is one gene. A gene is just a section of DNA.

Each gene is like a chemical message that tells your cells what to do.

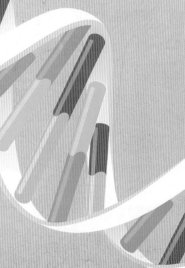

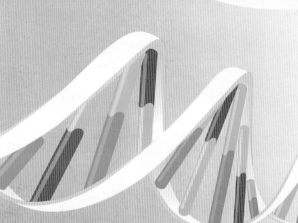

Internet link

For a link to a website where you'll find facts, games and activities about genes, go to **www.usborne-quicklinks.com**

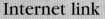

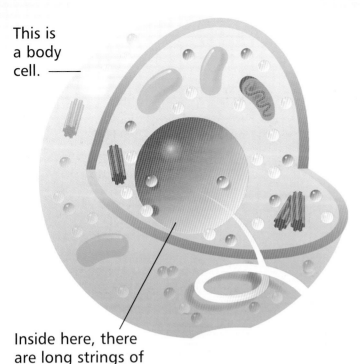

This is a body cell. ——

Inside here, there are long strings of DNA. Each string contains hundreds of genes.

In the family

Your genes come from your parents. You get half of your genes from your mum and the other half from your dad. That's why you probably look a little like them.

If both your parents are tall, you will probably be tall too when you grow up.

★

★

Some illnesses get passed on in genes. Scientists are doing experiments to find genes that don't work properly and replace them with healthy ones.

You and your genes

Your genes are special. Nobody else in the world has genes exactly like yours – unless you're an identical twin.

These two girls are identical twins. They look the same because they have exactly the same genes.

Babies

Babies come from inside their mothers. They grow there for about nine months, until they're big enough to live in the outside world.

Making a baby

You need two people to make a baby – a man and a woman. Inside the woman's body are lots of little round cells, called eggs. Inside the man's body are tiny, tadpole-shaped cells, called sperm.

The sperm swim into the woman's body. When one sperm joins up with an egg, a baby starts to grow.

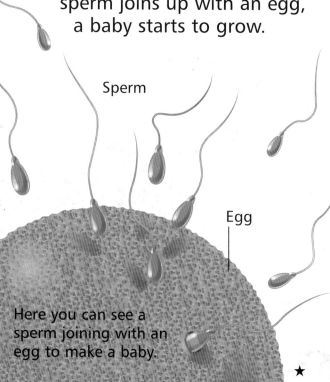

Sperm

Egg

Here you can see a sperm joining with an egg to make a baby.

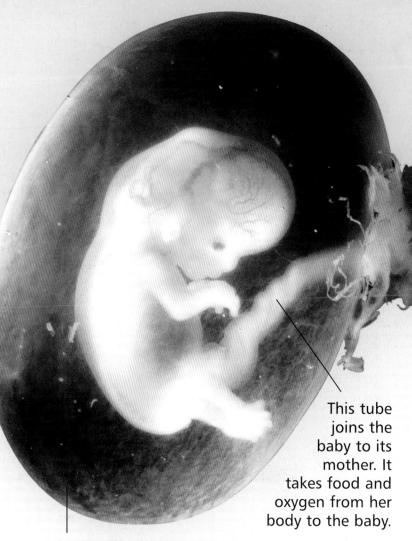

This tube joins the baby to its mother. It takes food and oxygen from her body to the baby.

Watery liquid

This baby has been growing inside its mother's tummy for eight weeks. It is only the size of a strawberry.

In the womb

Inside the woman's tummy is a stretchy bag, called her womb. This is where the baby grows. The womb is filled with warm, watery liquid that keeps the baby safe.

This shows a baby inside its mother's womb. The womb stretches as the baby grows.

Growing and moving

After about four months, the unborn baby has grown to the size of a lemon. Sometimes, the mother can feel the baby kicking inside her.

Womb

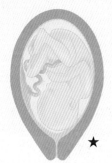

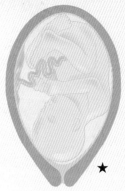

At four months, an unborn baby looks like this.

At six months, the baby is about 22cm (8½in) long.

At nine months, the baby is ready to be born.

Being born

When the baby is ready to be born, its mother's womb starts to squeeze. This pushes the baby out. It comes out of an opening between its mother's legs. It can take many hours for the baby to be born.

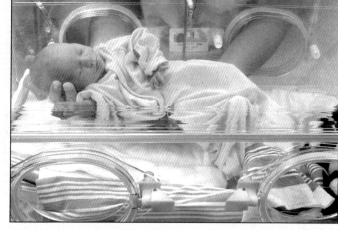

Sometimes, babies are born too early. Early babies need special care. This baby is being kept warm in a box called an incubator.

Internet link

For a link to a website where you can see how you grew from one tiny cell, go to **www.usborne-quicklinks.com**

This baby is just a few hours old. Newborn babies sleep for about 20 hours a day.

Growing and changing

Your body is getting bigger all the time. It keeps on growing from the time you are born until you're about 20 years old.

Changing shape

Each year, you grow about 6cm (2½in) taller. Some of your bones grow faster than others. This means that your body changes shape as you grow up.

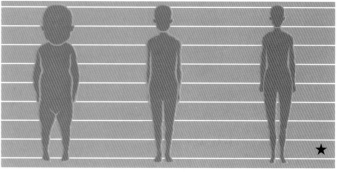

Babies have big heads compared with their bodies.

By seven, your body and legs have grown much longer.

Grown-ups have long legs. Their heads look small compared with their bodies.

As you grow, your bones get longer. Look at the bones in these two X-ray pictures.

This is the hand of a three-year-old.

This is a grown-up's hand.

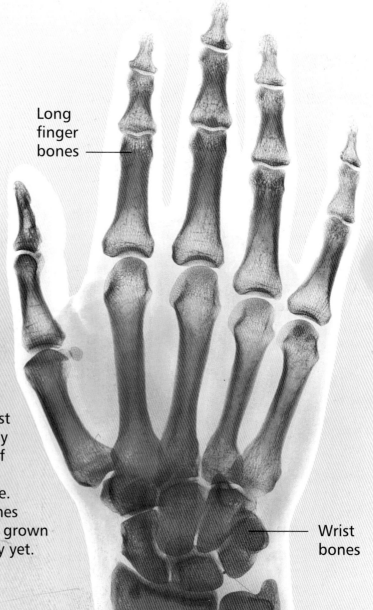

Long finger bones

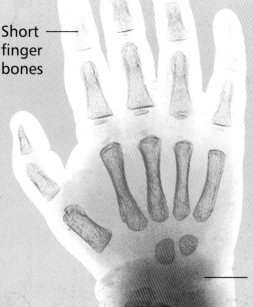

Short finger bones

The wrist is mostly made of bendy cartilage. The bones haven't grown properly yet.

Wrist bones

46

Learning and doing

Tiny babies can't do anything for themselves. Slowly, they learn to use their muscles, so they can sit up and crawl around. By the time they're two, most can walk and talk.

As you get older, you can learn to do more complicated things, such as balance on your hands.

Internet link

For a link to a website where you can do a fun activity to see how people change as they get older, go to
www.usborne-quicklinks.com

Getting old

As people grow old, their bodies get weaker. Their bones and muscles shrink and they get tired more easily.

By the time people are in their sixties, their hair has turned grey and their skin looks wrinkled.

Becoming an adult

Between the ages of about 10 and 18, lots of changes happen to your body. This time is called puberty. It's when you change from a child into an adult.

Girls' and boys' bodies change in different ways.

Boys' voices get deeper and their shoulders and chest get broader.

Boys grow hair on their faces.

Girls grow breasts.

Their hips get wider.

47

Staying healthy

You need to look after your body to keep it working properly. There are lots of things you can do to help your body stay healthy.

Try to eat a mixture of healthy foods. ★

Keeping fit

Exercising is an important way of keeping your body healthy, and it can be great fun too. Different kinds of exercise can help your body in different ways.

★

Some sports strengthen your heart and lungs, so you don't get out of breath so easily.

★

Some sports make your muscles stronger, so they can work harder without getting tired.

★

Other sports keep your joints bendy and stop you from getting stiff.

Swimming is a great way to exercise. It's good for your heart, lungs and muscles – and it keeps your joints bendy.

Internet link

For a link to a website where you can do lots of activities that show you how to stay healthy and safe, go to **www.usborne-quicklinks.com**

No worries

Worrying about things can make you feel ill. If you're worried about anything, it's a good idea to tell someone you trust, such as your mum, dad or teacher.

Time for bed

It's very important to get enough sleep. While you're asleep, your body has a chance to rest and repair itself. Your brain slows down, but it doesn't stop working. It uses the time to sort and store information.

Talking about problems can make you feel better.

Some scientists think that dreams are your brain's way of sorting through what's happened to you during the day.

Playing is fun, but it's good for you too. It helps you relax.

Keeping clean

If germs get inside you, they can make you ill. Washing helps to stop germs from spreading. You should always wash your hands before eating and after going to the toilet.

Healthy eating

You need to eat a mixture of foods to stay healthy. That's because different foods contain different things that your body needs.

This stir-fry contains a healthy mixture of foods – lots of rice and vegetables, some chicken and a little fat.

Internet link

For a link to a website where you can find out more about healthy eating, play lots of games and read some food riddles, go to **www.usborne-quicklinks.com**

Food groups

Some kinds of food give you energy to move around. Others help you to grow and to get better if you hurt yourself. This picture is a guide to how much of each kind of food you should eat every day.

Eat only small amounts of fatty or sugary foods, such as butter, cakes, sweets and sugary drinks.

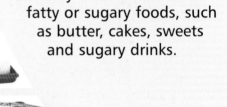

Eat two servings of food from the milk group, such as milk, yogurt and cheese. These foods make your bones strong.

The meat group includes fish, eggs, nuts and beans. These foods help you grow. Try to eat two servings a day.

Eat five servings of fruit and vegetables every day. You can have fresh, canned, dried or juiced fruit.

★

The grain group includes bread, pasta, rice and cereals. These foods give you energy. Try to eat six servings each day.

Food extras

The food you eat contains special chemicals that keep your body working properly. They're called vitamins and minerals. If you eat a good mixture of foods, you should get all the vitamins and minerals you need.

Oranges, strawberries and raspberries have vitamin C in them. This helps you get better when you're ill.

A mineral called calcium helps your bones to grow. Milk, yogurt and cheese contain lots of calcium.

Carrots, apricots and nectarines contain vitamin A, which keeps your eyes healthy.

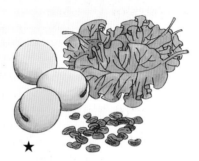

Iron is a mineral that keeps your blood healthy. You can get it from apricots, raisins and green vegetables.

Vitamin B helps your body to make energy. There's lots of it in wholemeal bread and brown rice.

If you feel hungry, try snacking on some fruit. It's a great way to get your vitamins.

Using food

When you eat, your body uses the food to make energy. But if you eat more food than you need, your body stores it as fat. That's why people get fatter if they eat a lot and don't exercise much.

Germs

Germs are everywhere. Usually, they don't do any harm. But some kinds can make you ill if they get inside you.

Germs can get into your body when you cut yourself. You can kill them by cleaning a cut with antiseptic liquid.

What are germs?

Germs are tiny living things that carry illnesses. Some travel through the air and some live in food or water. Others get passed on when people cough or sneeze. There are two main kinds of germs – bacteria and viruses.

These bacteria make your throat sore. They're shown 50,000 times bigger than they really are.

These bacteria give you tummy ache and make you feel sick.

These viruses give you a cold.

Washing your hands with hot, soapy water helps to stop germs from spreading.

Cooking food properly kills any germs that are living inside it.

Fighting germs

Your body can fight off some germs by itself. Special white cells in your blood hunt down germs and kill them. Some white blood cells make chemicals that kill germs. Others gobble the germs up.

Here you can see a white blood cell swallowing a germ.

Germ

White blood cell

This girl is having an injection, called an immunization. Immunizations protect you from dangerous germs that could make you very ill.

Internet link

For a link to a website where you can play lots of games to find out more about germs, go to **www.usborne-quicklinks.com**

Friendly bacteria

Not all bacteria are bad. Inside your tummy, you have millions and millions of bacteria that are actually good for you. They help to break down your food. They even make some of the vitamins that you need.

These are some of the bacteria that live inside your tummy.

Seeing a doctor

When you're ill, you may need to see a doctor. A doctor's job is to find out what's wrong with you and tell you what to do to get better.

Finding out

The doctor asks how you are feeling and checks your body for signs of illness. Here are some of the ways a doctor can find out what's wrong with you. Don't worry – these things don't hurt at all.

This doctor is using an instrument called a stethoscope to listen to a child's breathing and heartbeat.

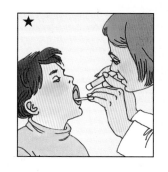

The doctor may ask you to open your mouth, so she can see if your throat looks red and sore.

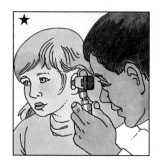

The doctor uses an instrument called an auriscope to look inside your ears.

Making it better

Often, the best way to get better is just to rest. Sometimes, you may have to take some medicine too. Medicines make illnesses better, but they can be dangerous. You should never take any medicine by yourself – always ask a grown-up first.

You often take medicine by drinking it in a liquid or by swallowing some pills.

These pills are called painkillers. They stop your body from hurting while you get better.

Medicine for sore eyes is often a liquid that's dropped into your eye.

Some medicine comes in a cream that you can rub into your skin.

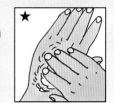

Medicines called antibiotics cure illnesses, such as sore throats, that are caused by bacteria inside your body.

These are capsules. They have powdery medicine inside them.

Internet link

For a link to a website where you can find out more about doctors, medicines and staying healthy, go to **www.usborne-quicklinks.com**

Treating injuries

If you hurt part of your body, the doctor may put on a bandage or a dressing. Dressings keep cuts and burns clean until your skin heals.

Bandages hold dressings in place. They're also used to support injured joints.

Looking inside

Sometimes, doctors need to see inside your body to find out what's wrong with you. They have some amazing machines to help them do this.

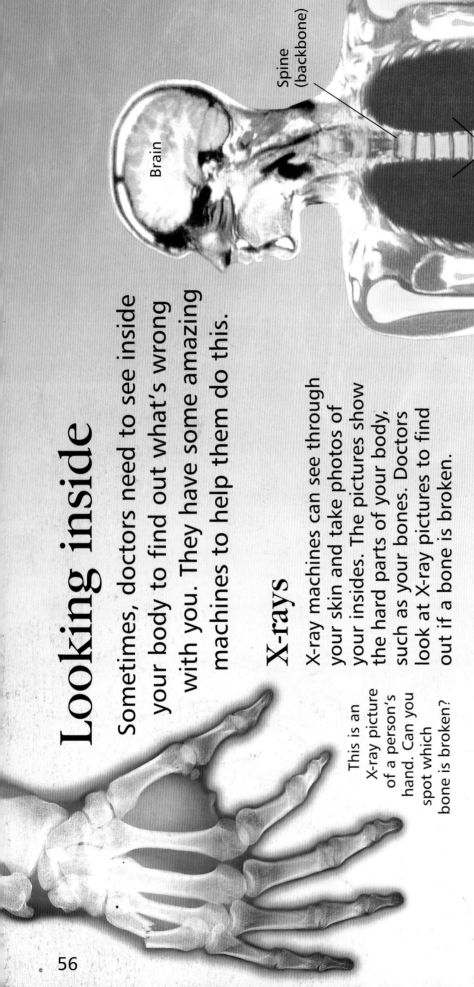

Brain

Spine (backbone)

Lungs

Kidneys

X-rays

X-ray machines can see through your skin and take photos of your insides. The pictures show the hard parts of your body, such as your bones. Doctors look at X-ray pictures to find out if a bone is broken.

This is an X-ray picture of a person's hand. Can you spot which bone is broken?

Scans

Machines called scanners let doctors see the soft parts of your body, as well as your bones. The scanner takes lots of different pictures. Then a computer puts all the pictures together, so doctors can get a detailed view of your insides.

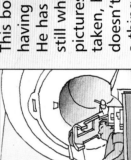

★ This boy is having a scan. He has to lie still while the pictures are taken, but he doesn't feel a thing.

This picture was made by a kind of scanner called an MRI scanner. It shows inside the body of a man.

—Thigh-bone

—Shinbone

Each hand is made up of 27 different bones.

Moving pictures

Ultrasound scans show up as fuzzy, moving pictures on a kind of TV screen. Doctors can use the scans to look at an unborn baby inside its mother's tummy.

★

The pictures show up here.

This woman is having an ultrasound scan. A doctor moves the scanner over her tummy.

This is an ultrasound scan of an unborn baby.

Baby's head

Mini cameras

To get a really good look, doctors can even put a tiny camera right inside a person's body. The camera is on the end of a thin tube, called an endoscope. It sends moving pictures from inside the body to a special TV screen.

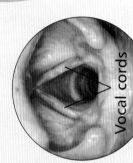

Vocal cords

This picture was taken with an endoscope. It shows the vocal cords inside a person's throat.

Internet link

For a link to a website where you can read about what it's like to have different kinds of scans, go to **www.usborne-quicklinks.com**

Going to a hospital

If you hurt yourself or if a part of your body isn't working properly, you might have to go to a hospital. The doctors and nurses who work there can cure lots of different illnesses.

Emergency!

If you get ill very suddenly or are hurt in an accident, you may need help quickly. The part of a hospital that deals with accidents and sudden illnesses is called Accident and Emergency, or A and E.

Internet link

For a link to a website where you can visit a hospital and find out what happens when someone has an operation, go to **www.usborne-quicklinks.com**

You may have to go to A and E if you break a bone or cut yourself badly.

People who are very ill are sometimes taken to A and E in an ambulance.

In and out

You don't always have to stay in hospital overnight. Often, you just go to see a doctor or nurse and come home the same day. This is called being an outpatient.

This girl is having a kind of treatment called physiotherapy. She is doing special exercises to make her muscles stronger.

This exercise stretches the girl's arm and shoulder muscles.

Having an operation

Sometimes, the best way to make you better is to open up your body and fix your insides. This is called an operation. A doctor who carries out operations is called a surgeon.

Before an operation, you're given some medicine to make you sleep. During the operation you don't feel a thing.

These doctors and nurses are carrying out an operation. The operation takes place in a room called an operating theatre.

Everything in the theatre has to be kept very clean.

Getting better

If you have an operation, you may need to stay in hospital for a few days afterwards. The nurses will look after you until you're better.

While you're in hospital, someone from your family can stay with you all the time.

The doctors and nurses wear special gowns and masks so they don't spread any germs.

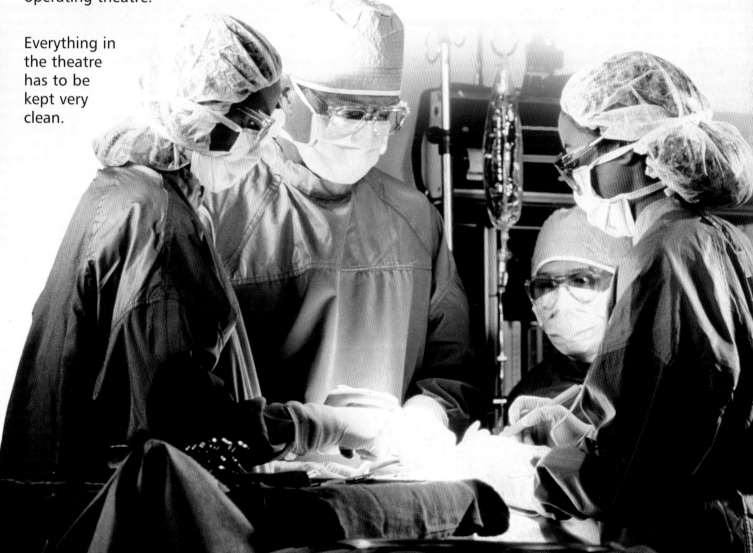

Body words

These pages explain some of the words you will find in this book and in other books about the human body.

anaesthetic medicine that makes you sleep or stops you from feeling pain during an operation.

artery a blood vessel that carries blood away from your heart to the rest of your body.

bacteria tiny living things that are too small to see. Some kinds can make you ill if they get inside you.

balanced diet a healthy mixture of different foods.

blood vessel a tube that carries blood around your body.

carbohydrate a chemical in food, such as bread, rice and pasta, that gives your body energy.

carbon dioxide a gas made by your body's cells. You get rid of it when you breathe out.

cartilage a material like bone, but softer, smoother and bendier.

cell a tiny living unit. Your body is made up of millions of cells. Most of them are much too small to see.

digestion the way your body breaks down food into chemicals it can use.

enamel a hard, white material that covers the outside of your teeth.

energy the strength to move around and do things. You get your energy from the food you eat.

gene one of the instructions that tell your body how to work and what shape to grow. You get your genes from your parents.

germs tiny living things that carry illnesses. They can make you ill if they get inside your body.

gland a part of your body that makes chemicals your body needs to work properly.

hormone a chemical messenger that travels around in your blood. Hormones tell different parts of your body what to do.

joint a part of your skeleton where two or more bones meet.

ligament a tough strap that holds two bones together.

melanin a brown colouring in skin and hair. Melanin protects your skin from sunlight. It also gives your skin and hair its colour.

minerals chemicals in food that your body needs to work properly. Fruit, vegetables, fish, nuts and milk all have minerals in them.

mucus a slimy liquid made by some parts of your body, such as your nose. Mucus helps to trap dirt and germs that you breathe in.

nerve a string-like bundle of cells that carries messages between your brain and your body.

neuron a nerve cell. Your brain and nerves are made of neurons.

optician someone who tests your eyes and supplies you with glasses or contact lenses if you need them.

organ a body part, such as your heart, lungs, eyes, liver or brain.

oxygen a gas that all your body's cells need to stay alive. You breathe in oxygen from the air around you.

pore a tiny hole in your skin. Sweat comes out of pores.

pregnant A woman who is pregnant has a baby growing inside her tummy.

protein a chemical in food, such as fish, meat and eggs, that helps your body to grow and repair itself.

puberty the time between the ages of about 10 and 18, when you change from a child into an adult.

senses the different ways you find out about the world around you. You have five senses – seeing, hearing, smell, taste and touch.

skeleton the framework of bones that holds you up and protects your insides.

skull the bony part of your head that protects your brain.

sweat a salty liquid made by your skin when you get hot.

temperature how hot or cold your body is. Your body's temperature is usually around 37°C (98.6°F).

tendon a tough strap that joins a muscle to a bone.

urine the pale yellow liquid that comes out when you go to the toilet. Urine is made inside your kidneys from water your body doesn't need.

vein a blood vessel that carries blood from your body back to your heart.

viruses tiny living things that carry illnesses. Colds and flu are caused by viruses.

vitamins chemicals in food, such as fresh fruit and vegetables, that your body needs to work properly.

X-ray a kind of photograph that shows the inside of your body.

Index

Acknowledgements

The publishers are grateful to the following for permission to reproduce material:

Key
t = top, m = middle, b = bottom, l = left, r = right

Cover, (blood cells) Science Photo Library, (chromosomes) BSIP, Ducloux/Science Photo Library, (children) Gary Buss/Getty Images; p1, Ron Chapple/Getty Images; p3, Dr. Arthur Tucker/Science Photo Library; pp4-5, Susumu Nishinaga/Science Photo Library; p6b, Mehau Kulyk/Science Photo Library; p7br, D. Phillips/Science Photo Library; p8bl, Omikron/Science Photo Library; p9tr, Oliver Strewe/Getty Images; p10tl, CNRI/Science Photo Library; p11tl, CNRI/Science Photo Library; p11br, ©Jose Luis Pelaez, Inc./CORBIS; p12br, ©Eric Crichton/CORBIS; p13tr, Omikron/Science Photo Library; p14bl, ©Chuck Keeler, Jr./CORBIS; p15t, ©Don Mason/CORBIS; p16tl, Andrew Syred/Science Photo Library; p17tr, Dr. Jeremy Burgess/Science Photo Library; p17b, Peter Cade/Getty Images; p18b, ©Lester V. Bergman/CORBIS; p19t, ©Roy Morsch/CORBIS; p20bl, Lunagrafix/Science Photo Library; p21r, Scott Camazine/Science Photo Library; p22r, ©Dimitri Lundt/CORBIS; p23r, Dr. Linda Stannard, UCT/Science Photo Library; p25m, CNRI/Science Photo Library; p25br, David Madison/Getty Images; p26b, Science Photo Library; p29tr, Science Photo Library; p29b, Jim Cummins/Getty Images; p30, (background) Creatas; p31tr, Alfred Pasieka/Science Photo Library; p31br, ©Roy Morsch/CORBIS; p32tr, International Stock/Robert Harding; p33br, Paul Arthur/Getty Images; p34bl, ©Laura Doss/CORBIS; p34tr, ©Jose Luis Pelaez, Inc./CORBIS; p35br, ©Tom Stewart/CORBIS; p36, (background) ©Digital Vision; p37br, Science Photo Library; p38bl, Peter Cade/Getty Images; p39tr, Biophoto Associates/Science Photo Library; p40bl, ©Gareth Brown/CORBIS; p40tr, ©Jose Luis Pelaez, Inc./CORBIS; p41r, Powerstock; p43br, ©Dennis Degnan/CORBIS; p44tr, Dr. G. Moscoso/Science Photo Library; p45mr, ©Lester Lefkowitz/CORBIS; p45b, ©Norbert Schaefer/CORBIS; p46b, Science Photo Library; p47tl, Alamy/ImageState; p47br, David Young-Wolff/Getty Images; p48b, David Madison/Getty Images; p49, ©Joyce Choo/CORBIS; p50tl, Jonelle Weaver/Getty Images; p51br, Anne Ackermann/Getty Images; p52ml, Custom Medical Stock Photo/Science Photo Library; p52br, Dr. Linda Stannard, UCT/Science Photo Library; p53tr, Biology Media/Science Photo Library; p53br, Custom Medical Stock Photo/Science Photo Library; p54b, Creatas; p55, (background) Creatas; p55t, Erich Schrempp/Science Photo Library; p55b, Alamy/GOODSHOOT; p56bl, Zephyr/Science Photo Library; pp56-57, Simon Fraser/Science Photo Library; p57m, CNRI/Science Photo Library; p57br, UHB Trust/Getty Images; p58, (background) Creatas; p58b, ©Tom Stewart/CORBIS; p59b, ©Pete Saloutos/CORBIS; pp60-61, (background) Creatas.

Cover design: Nicola Butler
Additional design: Stephanie Jones
Digital image manipulation: Stephanie Jones, Susie McCaffrey and John Russell
Additional editorial contributions: Rachel Firth, Sarah Khan and Claire Masset
Picture research: Claire Masset and Ruth King
Editor: Felicity Brooks
Art director: Mary Cartwright
Special thanks to Anna Claybourne and Sam Taplin

Every effort has been made to trace and acknowledge ownership of copyright. If any rights have been omitted, the publishers offer to rectify this in any subsequent editions following notification.